#LEADS to SALES tweet Book01

Creating Qualified Business Leads in the 21st Century

By Jim McAvoy
Foreword by Richard Whiteley

E-mail: info@thinkaha.com
20660 Stevens Creek Blvd., Suite 210,
Cupertino, CA 95014

Copyright © 2011 by Jim McAvoy

All rights reserved. No part of this book shall be reproduced, stored in a retrieval system, or transmitted by any means electronic, mechanical, photocopying, recording, or otherwise without written permission from the publisher.

Published by THiNKaha®, a Happy About® imprint
20660 Stevens Creek Blvd., Suite 210, Cupertino, CA 95014
http://thinkaha.com

First Printing: September 2011
Paperback ISBN: 978-1-61699-058-9 (1-61699-058-9)
eBook ISBN: 978-1-61699-059-6 (1-61699-059-7)
Place of Publication: Silicon Valley, California, USA
Paperback Library of Congress Number: 2011928301

Trademarks

All terms mentioned in this book that are known to be trademarks or service marks have been appropriately capitalized. Neither Happy About®, nor any of its imprints, can attest to the accuracy of this information. Use of a term in this book should not be regarded as affecting the validity of any trademark or service mark.

Warning and Disclaimer

Every effort has been made to make this book as complete and as accurate as possible. The information provided is on an "as is" basis. The author(s), publisher, and their agents assume no responsibility for errors or omissions. Nor do they assume liability or responsibility to any person or entity with respect to any loss or damages arising from the use of information contained herein.

Advance Praise

"Jim McAvoy gets it and lives it. His true genius in opening doors leads our business-development efforts, making things happen that were previously unimaginable."

Foster Mobley, Ed.D., Chief Executive Officer, The Foster Mobley Group

"The students [The University of Chicago Booth School of Business] just love your informative, easy-going guest-lecture style and the way you answer questions in a way that they really understand as it relates to creating qualified leads. THANKS SO MUCH. You are a critical part of my Entrepreneurial Selling course that is now rated as one of the top ten courses in the country by Inc. Magazine, 2011.

I am delighted that you have written this book and harnessed your entrepreneurial spirit within your declared major of lead-generation and prospecting. No doubt, sales professionals and business leaders across all industries will create more leads, relationships, and revenue as a result of reading your book."

Craig Wortmann, CEO, SalesEngine; Clinical Associate Professor, The University of Chicago Booth School of Business; Author, *What's Your Story*

"We enjoyed a productive multi-year relationship that resulted in a clear positive Return-on-Investment for our business. Throughout our partnership, Jim's knowledge of the healthcare sector was both evident and useful and helped accelerate our success. Jim's professional persistence with our prospects was also consistently recognized; this provided that vital positive first impression of our corporate brand. It is important to note that Jim methodically built and cultivated a database that we viewed as invaluable and will help us for future marketing campaigns. In summary, I strongly recommend reading Jim's book and following his insights and recommendations without hesitation."

John J. Scholl, CLU, ChFC, AAI, REBC, Area President, Gallagher Benefit Services, Inc., (A Division of Arthur J. Gallagher & Co.)

"I have worked with Jim on two separate occasions in which the sales teams needed a thorough jump-start to a higher win-rate. Because of Jim's experience and persistence, we accomplished our sales goals. And, in each situation, the skills, knowledge, and optimistic energy Jim exhibited not only raised the level of performance with all of us who had the fortune to work with him, but inspired us to enjoy all stages of the sales cycle. Jim is a consummate sales professional and the concepts provided in this book will help any sales professional make his/her numbers."

Tim Hawk, Principal, Boston Search Group Team Ventures

"Jim has directly supported the growth of our business. Jim's singular ability is to find joy in matching a prospective client with a vendor who can address a real need. Jim has taken the "cold" out of "cold calling."

He applies a principled approach, seeking a genuine match between vendor and prospective customer. This works because it is genuine and is focused on the customer's interests, not the vendor's. Prospects quickly sense Jim's authenticity and they respond to his friendly, open, and optimistic manner.

Jim's sales process starts on a golden note that reflects very well on us. I cannot imagine how anyone could have a better process or attitude for generating qualified sales calls. Buy this book; it shares Jim's insight and secrets. Your top line will thank you."

William Spencer, Principal, Whole-System Learning

"It is a rare gift to have access to the secrets of a sales superstar. The wisdom Jim McAvoy shares in this book shows the keen instincts, principles, polish, and congeniality that has made him a great success. These insights will not only help you turn Leads to Sales, but also help shape your marketing strategy and the overall effectiveness of your business."

Erik Van Slyke, Managing Director, Solleva Group

Dedication

To my lovely wife, Karen, and to our three wonderful children: Sally, Scott, and Leah. Thank you for your collective support and daily inspiration.

Acknowledgments

I would like to give a special thank you to my brother-in-law Philip for all of his time and guidance in writing this book. There are so many other people to thank for helping shape and advance this lead-generation offering, so to avoid leaving out anyone's name, let me say "thanks" to everyone with whom I have had the privilege to work over the years.

Why Did I Write This Book?

I wrote this book for the following three reasons.

1. To help others. I view this opportunity as a chance to give back and share what I have learned and experienced during my career.
2. The THiNKaha series is such a fun concept. The creative format appealed to me much more than lobbing out complicated models and charts that would likely glaze the eyes of my readers.
3. The realization of this book is a combination of personal fulfillment and the achievement of a goal, in addition to proof that dreams can come true if you trust your gut and pursue your own path fueled by an endless spring of passion.

Jim McAvoy
Office: 610-374-2443
Website: www.mcavoyleads.com
Email: jim@mcavoyleads.com

Creating Qualified Business Leads in the 21st Century

Contents

Foreword by Richard Whiteley	13
Section I Introduction/Context	17
Section II Lay Out Your Plan	29
Section III Evaluate Your Prospects	37
Section IV-A Approach the Gatekeeper	53
Section IV-B Approach the Executive	69
Section V Dialogue with Your Contact	83

Section VI Successfully Collaborate	107
Section VII Campaigns	113
Section VIII Conclusion and Path Forward	119
Appendix A Principles Are Important	123
Appendix B Favorite Quotation	133
About the Author	135

Foreword by Richard Whiteley

Have you ever stopped to consider?

Creating highly qualified sales leads is one of the most critical core competencies of any business. Not doing this always leads to failure.

One of the greatest wastes in selling is an accomplished sales person not getting maximum face time with prospects for lack of enough leads.

An even worse waste is when that sales person actually makes the face-to-face call only to find the lead is unqualified...a complete bust!

In the hands of a talented sales force, qualified leads will ensure a company's ability to set and meet aggressive growth targets.

Face-to-face skills win business from your prospects. Good admin skills help you find them. Discover ways to maximize one and minimize the other.

What is the ratio of your face-to-face time to your prep time? What should it be?

Foreword by Richard Whiteley

#LEADS to SALES Tweet deals with these critical lead generation issues and offers 140 tips that can be adapted to virtually any sales situation.

Jim McAvoy understands these issues better than anyone I know. He has made qualified lead generation the core expertise of his practice.

I have known Jim since he was creating leads in my company almost 20 years ago. Since then this has become both his love and his "turf."

You will find the wisdom Jim has gained over the years and presented in sound bite form to be practical, powerful, and profitable.

Enjoy the book and make it work for you.

Richard Whiteley
Entrepreneur
Award-winning Author, *The Customer-Driven Company*
and Co-Author, *Customer-Centered Growth*
Co-Founder, The Forum Corporation
Principal, The Whiteley Group

Section I: Introduction/Context

Section I
Introduction/Context

Question: What do "gargling bleach," "crawling over broken glass," and "having a root canal done without Novocain" all have in common?

Answer: These are all activities that high-performing sales professionals have claimed they would do rather than spend time cold-calling and focusing on lead generation–related activities.

Section I: Introduction/Context

1

Companies of all sizes, in all sectors, consistently grapple with top-line and bottom-line growth.

2

Highly paid sales professionals are hired to advance relationships, close deals, and bring in revenue.

3

Sales professionals consistently acknowledge that the initial step in most sales processes is prospecting.

4

The skills and time of sales professionals are better spent pursuing business from qualified leads rather than cold-calling.

5

Prospecting is like doing daily sit-ups and push-ups. Everyone knows they are good for you, yet most people do not want to do them.

6

Reserve and protect specific times during the week for prospecting—otherwise you will likely find time to avoid it.

Section I: Introduction/Context

7

Start small: Block off fifteen minutes one day per week to concentrate on prospecting. Build up to forty minutes five times per week.

8

Set short-term goals of having a certain number of substantive conversations per week.

9

Reward yourself for achieving small milestones such as conducting a specific number of meaningful calls per day or week.

10

Possessing the attitude and belief that you are being helpful and supportive by introducing your product or service is paramount.

Section I: Introduction/Context

11

A combination of thick skin and a short-term memory are necessary given the high level of rejection you will receive.

12

Be willing to start small via a crawl-walk-run model that begins with a three-month pilot.

13

Become a utility that a firm can't imagine living without.

14

Remain open and receptive to new ideas and tools.

Section I: Introduction/Context

15

Continuously build and advance the reservoir of future prospects to approach.

16

Stop trying to sell. Give people the opportunity to buy.

17

Make your offering simple to understand and easy to buy.

Section II: Lay Out Your Plan

Section II
Lay Out Your Plan

The contracting phase introduces tools that help provide clarity and focus to your universe of available prospects. Laying out the plan helps you advance your strategy and understand the associated trade-offs involved when selecting specific prospects you choose to pursue.

18

Basic data should include a potential client's industry, location, and size in terms of revenue or number of employees.

19

Typically, there are multiple buying centers within each firm. Consider approaching many of them.

20

The sales funnel of probability shapes the volume of prospects needed to hit desired revenue targets.

21

Identify 200 qualified names—contacts that are potential buyers.

Section II: Lay Out Your Plan

22

Each prospect of 200 has one potential need for your service per year, and you are on the short list for 10% of them.

23

Out of twenty qualified opportunities, you can assume the probability of closing on 10% of these.

24

Strive for unsighted wins per year. This unforeseen revenue will help you make your numbers.

25

A strong lead-generation plan will increase your probability of establishing new dialogues resulting in additional pipeline situations.

Section II: Lay Out Your Plan

26

Closing non-forecasted revenue will boost your chances of achieving your goals for the next month, quarter, and/or year.

27

Agree what success will look like in the first three to four months of a new assignment.

28

Create an environment where you know if you are winning or advancing on a weekly basis.

Section III: Evaluate Your Prospects

Section III
Evaluate Your Prospects

Take time to make sure that all of your information is correct. It shows that you put time and effort into knowing about the prospect's company and their business issues. The Master Database is introduced and serves as a pivotal tool in collecting and managing data.

Section III: Evaluate Your Prospects

29

Preliminary research and evaluation form the fundamental basis of knowledge of the prospect.

30

Baseline data includes the company's contact information (telephone and e-mail), physical address, and website address.

31

It is important to visit the firm's website for specific contact data for individual decision-makers and their titles.

32

Quality over quantity. A few well-researched leads far outweigh a large number of unqualified leads.

33

Integrate your cold-calling with warm-calling. Approach qualified cold accounts and revisit warm "alumni" firms and contacts.

34

Utilize web-based search tools and social media sites to locate former clients with whom you had successful interactions.

35

Blend both a reactive and proactive lead-generation strategy.

Section III: Evaluate Your Prospects

36

Employ online tools and search engines to help target future clients and gather necessary contact data.

37

Verify if your prospect runs on a calendar year or fiscal year. This information will guide the messaging and timing of your approach.

38

View industry publications for the comings and goings of key personnel you are targeting.

Section III: Evaluate Your Prospects

39

Calls are made to validate the executive's role and to begin the positive dialogue with his/her assistant (otherwise known as the gatekeeper).

40

It is important to gather the correct pronunciations, direct phone numbers, and e-mail addresses for the executive and assistant.

41

All vital data is centrally gathered on the Master Database, a methodical list of prospects that serves to promote focus and direction.

Section III: Evaluate Your Prospects

42

One must attain a fundamental understanding of the prospect's leading business issues and link them to your product or service.

43

Review the chairman's message in the annual report along with highlights from the most recent quarterly report.

Section III: Evaluate Your Prospects

44

Ask former and current clients for referrals.

45

Peruse the targeted firm's online press releases and relevant news to identify the arrival of new prospects to contact.

46

Read over your prospect's online biography, if available, to identify potential connection points.

Section III: Evaluate Your Prospects

47

Cut and paste all relevant online links, including the company website, onto the Master Database.

48

Batching qualified prospects in groups of five to ten helps to make the process seem less overwhelming.

49

Storytelling is a pivotal skill. Learn your firm's success stories and share them with your potential prospects.

Section IV-A: Approach the Gatekeeper

Section IV-A
Approach the Gatekeeper

This is the moment of truth. Here is where you lay out a strategy that includes multiple types of deliberate and intentional approaches in various combinations. The importance of documentation continues as the Master Database is used as a central depository to keep track of progress made with scores of prospects.

Section IV-A: Approach the Gatekeeper

50

A core component of your success will depend on your ability to connect with the gatekeeper (in essence, the executive assistant).

51

Is the gatekeeper friend or foe? That depends on your approach.

52

The word gatekeeper often conjures up emotions of anxiety, frustration, and disappointment. Relax and get rid of preconceived notions.

Section IV-A: Approach the Gatekeeper

53

Many will attest that trying to curry favor with the executive assistant is daunting at best.

54

Offer the executive assistant respect and appreciation.

55

Recognize that assistants are typically very smart and intuitive. There is a reason why they are working with these senior executives.

Section IV-A: Approach the Gatekeeper

56

Ask the assistant or executive if he/she has a brief moment to talk when you first make contact.

57

The goal is to successfully engage the executive gatekeeper in a mutually positive and productive dialogue.

58

Politely ask the assistant to clarify your missing or outdated information. Formulate questions based on your current data.

Section IV-A: Approach the Gatekeeper

59

A friendly and understanding tone is required, along with patience, as you try to establish a positive rapport with the gatekeeper.

60

If the gatekeeper instructs you to send the e-mail to her/him and not to the executive, do as you are told and do not try to outsmart them.

61

Ignore incoming calls if on a call, and offer to be placed on hold if you hear the beep on a prospect's line.

Section IV-A: Approach the Gatekeeper

62

A cheerful attitude and prepared approach will increase the odds of accessing a gatekeeper's assistance.

63

The goal is to establish high trust and a positive rapport.

64

Trust may be defined as the residue of promises kept.

Section IV-A: Approach the Gatekeeper

65

One must be solid and authentic to have a chance, and most gatekeepers can quickly detect when someone is a prepared professional.

66

The gatekeeper can sense when someone is a fast-talking charlatan pretending to have false referrals.

67

Bottom line: No one likes a glad-hander. Be genuine, and mean it.

Section IV-A: Approach the Gatekeeper

68

The "boomerang of honesty" will eventually surface (it always does) as a positive approach often begets a positive result.

69

If the executive is busy, have the assistant transfer you to a colleague. They often pick up when they see their associate's phone number.

70

Your words and attitude should reflect a "spirit of appreciation," resulting in an effective interaction.

Section IV-B: Approach the Executive

Section IV-B
Approach the Executive

Making a connection with key decision makers is what you strive for after all of your hard work. Be confident and apply all the knowledge that you have gained in the lead-generation process. Go for it!

Section IV-B: Approach the Executive

71

It is vital to confirm the correct pronunciation and spelling of the names for the gatekeeper and executive.

72

Listen—remember the ratio of two ears and one mouth.

73

Given the existence of caller ID, avoid calling over and over again.

Section IV-B: Approach the Executive

74

Keep your comments short and sweet when you talk, and avoid rambling at all costs.

75

You may consider creating a short outline to make your salient points.

76

Most people can detect, and dislike, someone reading verbatim from a script—so be mindful of speaking naturally.

77

A successful approach is a combination of elementary psychology, business acumen, and good manners.

78

Ask and answer the question of what makes your firm unique from the prospect's perspective.

79

Create and share a partial client list in your introductory e-mail to build credibility and provide assurance.

80

A written client testimonial that's relevant to a prospect's business is often very useful.

Section IV-B: Approach the Executive

81
Concise case studies are valuable, outlining the articulated business challenge and the result you helped them achieve.

82
When someone offers a lead, be careful not to overstate the source when making the initial contact to avoid misrepresentation.

83

The initial e-mail needs to succinctly introduce your firm and convey an appreciation of the executive's business priorities.

Section IV-B: Approach the Executive

84

Read your e-mail out loud for flow.

85

Proofread all correspondence to ensure that there are no spelling or grammatical errors.

86

A follow-up e-mail may be sent within one to four weeks if no reply is received.

87

Use color to help sort and prioritize your lead generation efforts in your Master Database.

Section IV-B: Approach the Executive

88

Brevity matters. E-mails must be compatible to hand-held devices, meaning you have about 5 to 10 seconds to get your point across.

89

Voicemail messages should be succinct. Speak slowly and clearly.

90

The importance of documentation continues as the Master Database is used as a central depository to track the progress with your prospects.

Section V: Dialogue with Your Contact

Section V
Dialogue with Your Contact

This step emphasizes counterintuitive concepts, necessitates asking a few high-impact questions, and utilizes a model focusing on professional courtesy and connecting with the prospect in a value-added and respectful manner.

Section V: Dialogue with Your Contact

91

Make the first call and get over that potential barrier. You will likely discover that it is not as bad as crawling over broken glass.

92

In many situations, you will be the first touchpoint for your firm, or what we call the brand ambassador.

93

Call between 7:30 and 8 a.m. and 5 and 6 p.m. because assistants are typically not in the office to intercept calls.

Section V: Dialogue with Your Contact

94

If you are calling in multiple time zones, set up your day accordingly to take advantage of the best times to call.

95

Stay off the phone if your energy level is low.

96

A demonstration of empathy for your prospect's busy schedule holds unforeseen emotional sway.

Section V: Dialogue with Your Contact

97

Avoid using a cell phone to prospect. Possible dropped calls and poor reception may lead to a negative first impression.

98

Let prospects hear the smile in your voice when you are on the phone.

99

Strive to make indelible impressions with every prospect interaction.

Section V: Dialogue with Your Contact

100

Apologize if you unintentionally upset or disturb a prospect.

101

Whenever possible, use day-to-day words and avoid "consultant speak."

102

Always be on time for scheduled calls.

103

Avoid pointing out a client's shortfalls—they already know about them. Instead, focus on conduits for success.

Section V: Dialogue with Your Contact

104

Keep the length of your first call as short as possible. The executive will appreciate your efficiency and ability to not waste time.

105

Once you connect with the prospect on the phone, quickly articulate the issues they are likely wrestling with now.

106

Basic gestures of courtesy are much appreciated and can go a long way in establishing a connection.

Section V: Dialogue with Your Contact

107

Adjust the approach to your audience based on their tone and word choice.

108

Share information and establish a dialogue with the goal of being helpful and supportive of a prospect's agenda.

109

An empathetic attitude will promote a level of understanding that will increase the chances of establishing a dialogue.

Section V: Dialogue with Your Contact

110

For better connectivity, try to visualize the prospect (whether or not an online headshot is available).

111

A prospect's request to receive information via letter or fax is not code for "go away." Follow their request.

112

If there is no initial response, keep the file open and follow up.

113

A bit of "soft tenacity" might be appreciated by the buyer, and a gentle nudge may help advance the sales process.

Section V: Dialogue with Your Contact

114

Utilizing a few short and thoughtful questions will serve you well.

115

Provide creative and practical options to help advance early-stage dialogues.

116

Listen hard! Honor the silence and provide your prospect with the space to think before answering each question.

117

Focus on understanding a prospect's priorities and concerns.

Section V: Dialogue with Your Contact

118

Be sure to understand their expectations for the follow-up call or meeting.

119

Take the high road and offer verbal respect to your competitors, if asked. Then redirect and clarify your edge over them.

120

Ask the prospect to articulate what intrigued them to pursue a follow-up call with you and your firm.

121

Qualifying out a prospect is helpful in the sense that you now know that there is not a fit and you can redirect to other targets.

Section V: Dialogue with Your Contact

122

Be willing to be "first in line" if they are currently being well served. Stand ready to be helpful when there is a need for your services.

123

If appropriate, ask your prospect what result needs to be achieved for him/her to collect a bonus, get promoted, or keep their job.

124

Another question to consider asking your prospect is what his/her boss would say are the vital priorities this year.

125

You do not need to endure a prospect's rudeness. If you caught them on a bad day, simply find a polite way to exit the call and move on.

126

Politely disengage if you determine that your contact does not have the influence to make a final decision on your proposal.

Section VI: Successfully Collaborate

Section VI
Successfully Collaborate

Like a successful baton handoff in a relay race, this phase focuses on how best to efficiently and effectively hand off a qualified lead to the assigned sales professional.

Section VI: Successfully Collaborate

127

Ascertain the resources within your firm that will efficiently follow up with a successful lead and advance the relationship.

128

Collaboration is critical to success. As they say, "Tigers hunt better in pairs."

129

Consider having one of your colleagues participate via telephone while you are meeting with a prospect.

Section VI: Successfully Collaborate

130

Send the initial follow-up e-mail within the first 24 hours to maintain any positive momentum.

131

Typically, small teams consisting of two to four people are more than enough to advance a qualified lead.

Section VII: Campaigns

Section VII
Campaigns

Creative marketing campaigns, if well conceived and implemented, can serve as a useful activity to help increase awareness in the marketplace.

Section VII: Campaigns

132

Include a $5 gift certificate from a national coffee chain along with a report, and ask them to review it while having a coffee on us.

133

Send a book or book summary that encourages a prospect to think about an approach that is in line with your firm's products or services.

134

Send your information via overnight service to demonstrate your sense of seriousness.

Section VII: Campaigns

135

Sticky notes, customized with the logo of your firm, are an effective giveaway and a good way to establish presence.

136

Hand-written correspondence on high-quality stationery adds a personal touch. The odds are higher that your message will be read.

137

Consider contacting your prospects every other month with something of potential interest. Awareness counts.

Section VIII: Conclusion and Path Forward

Section VIII
Conclusion and Path Forward

Feel confident. Form a plan of action and stick to it. This will lead you on the road to success.

Section VIII: Conclusion and Path Forward

138

With a well-executed lead-generation strategy, the painful days of cold-calling can be greatly reduced, if not eliminated completely.

139

The old sales approach is being superseded by a more productive, upfront plan of action.

140

You may now move forward more confidently with a renewed attitude and strategy, which will allow you to exceed your revenue goals.

Appendix A: Principles Are Important

Appendix A
Principles Are Important

Principles are a public declaration of a firm's DNA. This announces to the world what an enterprise stands for and how it is wired. They provide much more depth beyond banal platitudes such as "We care about our customers" and "Our employees are our most important asset."

Appendix A: Principles Are Important

A-1

The truth is that very few businesses have defined their principles, let alone displayed them to the marketplace.

A-2

Ideally, a firm's principles are conveyed in the actions and behaviors of the leadership team and employees.

A-3

The lack of either the existence or the articulation of defined principles presents a wonderful breakaway opportunity.

A-4

Serving customers—helping them compete and win—is a privilege.

A-5

Offer steadfast support, respect, and appreciation.

Appendix A: Principles Are Important

A-6

Loyalty, along with patience, is vital for enduring success.

A-7

Too many times we move too quickly and unintentionally damage the bonds that engender mutual respect.

A-8

Work with customers, wherever they are in their growth.

A-9

Inquire, don't persuade.

Appendix A: Principles Are Important

A-10

Build high-trust partnerships by talking openly and listening.

A-11

Give a little extra to delight customers.

A-12

Treat every customer as a potential reference.

Appendix B: Favorite Quotation

Appendix B
Favorite Quotation

"Nothing in the world can take the place of persistence. Talent will not; nothing is more common than unsuccessful men with talent. Genius will not; unrewarded genius is almost a proverb. Education will not; the world is full of educated derelicts. Persistence and determination alone are omnipotent. The slogan 'Press On' has solved and always will solve the problems of the human race."

Calvin Coolidge
30th President of the United States
(1872 - 1933)

About the Author

About the Author

Jim McAvoy, founder and president of JWMcAvoy & Company Ltd., has almost twenty-five years of experience maximizing sales results for clients in a wide range of industries from boutique firms to Fortune 500 companies. He has helped his clients secure $60 million of incremental revenue to date using his proven L.E.A.D.S.™ process for lead creation.

McAvoy holds a BA in Economics and History from the College of William & Mary. He also attained the Certified Employee Benefits Specialist (CEBS) designation, which is conferred by a partnership of the International Foundation of Employee Benefit Plans and the Wharton School of the University of Pennsylvania. Mr. McAvoy can be contacted at 610-374-2443 or jim@mcavoyleads.com

Other Books in the THiNKaha Series

The THiNKaha book series is for thinking adults who lack the time or desire to read long books, but want to improve themselves with knowledge of the most up-to-date subjects. THiNKaha is a leader in timely, cutting-edge books and mobile applications from relevant experts that provide valuable information in a fun, Twitter-brief format for a fast-paced world.

They are available online at http://thinkaha.com or at other online and physical bookstores.

1. *#BOOK TITLE tweet Book01:* 140 Bite-Sized Ideas for Compelling Article, Book, and Event Titles by Roger C. Parker
2. *#BUSINESS SAVVY PM tweet Book01:* Project Management Mindsets, Skills, and Tools for Generating Successful Business Results by Cinda Voegtli
3. *#COACHING tweet Book01:* 140 Bite-Sized Insights On Making A Difference Through Executive Coaching by Sterling Lanier
4. *#CONTENT MARKETING tweet Book01:* 140 Bite-Sized Ideas to Create and Market Compelling Content by Ambal Balakrishnan
5. *#CORPORATE CULTURE tweet Book01:* 140 Bite-Sized Ideas to Help You Create a High Performing, Values Aligned Workplace that Employees LOVE by S. Chris Edmonds
6. *#CROWDSOURCING tweet Book01:* 140 Bite-Sized Ideas to Leverage the Wisdom of the Crowd by Kiruba Shankar and Mitchell Levy
7. *#DEATHtweet Book01:* A Well-Lived Life through 140 Perspectives on Death and Its Teachings by Timothy Tosta
8. *#DEATH tweet Book02:* 140 Perspectives on Being a Supportive Witness to the End of Life by Timothy Tosta
9. *#DIVERSITYtweet Book01:* Embracing the Growing Diversity in Our World by Deepika Bajaj

#LEADS to SALES **tweet** Book01

10. *#DREAMtweet Book01:* Inspirational Nuggets of Wisdom from a Rock and Roll Guru to Help You Live Your Dreams by Joe Heuer
11. *#ENTRYLEVELtweet Book01:* Taking Your Career from Classroom to Cubicle by Heather R. Huhman
12. *#ENTRY LEVEL tweet Book02:* Relevant Advice for Students and New Graduates in the Day of Social Media by Christine Ruff and Lori Ruff
13. *#EXPERT EXCEL PROJECTS tweet:* Taking Your Excel Project From Start To Finish Like An Expert by Larry Moseley
14. *#IT OPERATIONS MANAGEMENT tweet Book01:* Managing Your IT Infrastructure in The Age of Complexity by Peter Spielvogel, Jon Haworth, Sonja Hickey
15. *#JOBSEARCHtweet Book01:* 140 Job Search Nuggets for Managing Your Career and Landing Your Dream Job by Barbara Safani
16. *#LEADERSHIPtweet Book01:* 140 Bite-Sized Ideas to Help You Become the Leader You Were Born to Be by Kevin Eikenberry
17. *#LEADS to SALES tweet Book01:* Creating Qualified Business Leads in the 21st Century by Jim McAvoy
18. *#LEAN SIX SIGMA tweet Book01:* Business Process Excellence for the Millennium by Dr. Shree R. Nanguneri
19. *#LEAN STARTUP tweet Book01:* 140 Insights for Building a Lean Startup! by Seymour Duncker
20. *#MILLENNIALtweet Book01:* 140 Bite-Sized Ideas for Managing the Millennials by Alexandra Levit
21. *#MOJOtweet:* 140 Bite-Sized Ideas on How to Get and Keep Your Mojo by Marshall Goldsmith
22. *#MY BRAND tweet Book01:* A Practical Approach to Building Your Personal Brand - 140 Characters at a Time by Laura Lowell
23. *#OPEN TEXTBOOK tweet Book01:* Driving the Awareness and Adoption of Open Textbooks by Sharyn Fitzpatrick
24. *#PARTNER tweet Book01:* 140 Bite-Sized Ideas for Succeeding in Your Partnerships by Chaitra Vedullapalli

25. *#PLAN to WIN tweet Book01:* Strategic Territory and Account Planning by Ron Snyder and Eric Doner
26. *#PRESENTATION tweet Book01:* 140 Ways to Present with Impact by Wayne Turmel
27. *#PRIVACY tweet Book01:* Addressing Privacy Concerns in the Day of Social Media by Lori Ruff
28. *#PROJECT MANAGEMENT tweet Book01:* 140 Powerful Bite-Sized Insights on Managing Projects by Guy Ralfe and Himanshu Jhamb
29. *#QUALITYtweet Book01:* 140 Bite-Sized Ideas to Deliver Quality in Every Project by Tanmay Vora
30. *#RISK MANAGEMENT tweet Book01:* Proactive Risk Management: Taming Alligators by Cinda Voegtli & Laura Erkeneff
31. *#SCRAPPY GENERAL MANAGEMENT tweet Book01:* Practical Practices for Magnificent Management Results by Michael Horton
32. *#SOCIAL MEDIA PR tweet Book01:* 140 Bite-Sized Ideas for Social Media Engagement by Janet Fouts
33. *#SOCIALMEDIA NONPROFIT tweet Book01:* 140 Bite-Sized Ideas for Nonprofit Social Media Engagement by Janet Fouts with Beth Kanter
34. *#SPORTS tweet Book01:* What I Learned from Coaches About Sports and Life by Ronnie Lott with Keith Potter
35. *#STANDARDS tweet Book01:* 140 Bite-Sized Ideas for Winning the Industry Standards Game by Karen Bartleson
36. *#TEAMWORK tweet Book01:* Lessons for Leading Organizational Teams to Success 140 Powerful Bite-Sized Insights on Lessons for Leading Teams to Success by Caroline G. Nicholl
37. *#THINKtweet Book01:* Bite-Sized Lessons for a Fast Paced World by Rajesh Setty
38. *#TOXINS tweet Book01:* 140 Easy Tips to Reduce Your Family's Exposure to Environmental Toxins by Laurel J. Standley Ph.D.

THiNK Continuity™ Training/Learning Program

THiNK Continuity™ delivers high-quality, cost-effective continuous learning in easy-to-understand, worthwhile, and digestible chunks. Fifteen minutes with a *THiNKaha®* book will allow the reader to have one or more "aha" moments. An hour and a half monthly with a THiNK Continuity program will allow the learner to have an opportunity to truly digest the topic being covered.

Offered online and/or in person, these engaging programs feature gurus (ours and yours) on such relevant topics as Leadership, Management, Sales, Marketing, Work-Life Balance, Project Management, Social Media and Networking, Presentation Skills, and other topics of your choosing. The "learning" audience, whether it is clients, employees, or partners, can now experience high-quality learning that will enhance your brand value and empower your company as a thought leader. This program fits a real need where time and the high cost of developing custom content are no longer an option for every organization.

Just **THiNK...**

- **C**ontinuous Employee/Client/Prospect Learning
- **O**ngoing Thought Leadership Development
- **N**otable Experts Presenting on Relevant Topics
- **T**ime Your Attendees Can Afford – 15 min. to 2 hrs/mth
- **I**nformation Delivered in Digestible Chunks
- **N**ame the Topic – We Help You Provide Expert Best Practices
- **U**nderstand and Implement the Takeaways
- **I**nternal Expertise Shared Externally
- **T**raining/Prospecting Cost Decreases, Effectiveness Increases
- **Y**ou Win, They Win!

www.ingramcontent.com/pod-product-compliance
Ingram Content Group UK Ltd.
Pitfield, Milton Keynes, MK11 3LW, UK
UKHW021303180426
11947UKWH00015B/989